# You, Unstuck

Other Books by Seth Adam Smith

*Your Life Isn't for You*

*Marriage Isn't for You*

# You, Unstuck

## You Are the Solution
## to Your Greatest Problem

### Seth Adam Smith

Berrett–Koehler Publishers, Inc.
*a BK Life book*

Berrett-Koehler Publishers, Inc.
1333 Broadway, Suite 1000
Oakland, CA 94612-1921
Tel: (510) 817-2277  Fax: (510) 817-2278  www.bkconnection.com

**Ordering Information**

**Quantity sales.** Special discounts are available on quantity purchases by corporations, associations, and others. For details, contact the "Special Sales Department" at the Berrett-Koehler address above.

**Individual sales.** Berrett-Koehler publications are available through most bookstores. They can also be ordered directly from Berrett-Koehler: Tel: (800) 929-2929; Fax: (802) 864-7626; www.bkconnection.com

**Orders for college textbook/course adoption use.** Please contact Berrett-Koehler: Tel: (800) 929-2929; Fax: (802) 864-7626

Berrett-Koehler and the BK logo are registered trademarks of Berrett-Koehler Publishers, Inc.

ISBN 978-1-62656-346-9

First Edition

2015        10 9 8 7 6 5 4 3 2 1

Cover design: Leslie Waltzer / Crowfoot Design
Cover art: Jeevan Sivasubramaniam
Author photo: Dmitry Ternovoy
Interior design and composition: Leigh McLellan Design
Copyediting: Elissa Rabellino

### Dedicated to

*Boyd Adams, my grandfather,*
*and Lyn Adams Smith, my mother,*
*for their never-ending faith and support.*

*You are the reason why I insist on*
*going by my full name.*

# *Contents*

## 1

## By the Beating of Our Own Wings

Over seven hundred years ago, an Italian poet by the name of Dante Alighieri wrote an epic poem entitled *Divine Comedy* —an allegorical representation of the soul's journey to (or away from) God.

The first part of the poem contains a chilling description of the nine circles of hell. As Dante figuratively descends these nine levels, he details the torture and agony of the souls he witnesses along the way.

In the ninth circle, the very depth and center of hell, Dante encounters Satan: a massive, terrifying beast with six wings and three nightmarish faces of different colors. Upon his back rests the entire vestibule of hell—and surrounding him is an element that we all fear and dread.

Hellfire?

No, there is no fire in Satan's level of torment.

According to Dante, instead of standing in the midst of fire, Satan is standing waist deep *in a lake of solid ice*.

If you think that's strange, wait until you read this:

> *The emperor of the realm of grief protruded*
> *From mid-breast up above the surrounding ice....*
>
> *If he was truly once as beautiful*
> *As he is ugly now, and raised his brows*
> *Against his Maker—then all sorrow may well...*
>
> *Two wings spread forth from under [his head]...*
>
> *Strong, and befitting such a bird, immense—*
> *I have never seen at sea so broad a sail—*
> *Unfeathered, batlike, and issuing three winds*
>
> *That went forth as he beat them, to freeze the whole*
> *Realm of [hell] that surrounded him.*
> *He wept with all [eyes], and the tears fell...*[1]

Did you catch that?

Satan's lake of ice—Satan's prison—is kept frozen *by the beating of his own wings.*

This is one of the most impressive ironies in literature because it symbolically illustrates three things: the isolation of hell, the stagnation of hell, and the fact that the isolation and stagnation of hell are *of our own making*. In his anger, frustration, and bitterness, Satan has sunk to the lowest levels of isolation. There, by the beating of his own wings, this fallen angel is "trapped," crushed under the weight of his own victims and mired in a frozen lake of victimhood.

You see, in Dante's *Inferno* (one of the three parts of *The Divine Comedy*), Satan has embraced the most damning philosophy of all time. This philosophy is contemptible and destructive, crushing hope and freezing its followers in a lake of stagnation. Instead of ennobling and strengthening those who embrace it, this belief drags men and women down. It encourages isolation, fosters fear, and perpetuates resentment. It robs men and women of their strength and will to fight; it makes them give in and fall down instead of holding true and standing up. Like a pernicious plague, this belief—if embraced—will stunt our growth and limit our life.

The philosophy?

*I can't change. I am a victim of my circumstances.*

And yet, for all its horrifying consequences, we nevertheless cling to this damning belief to one degree or another. To make it go down easier, we sugarcoat it with pleasing justifications and reassure ourselves that this belief will soothe our pains. And for a time, it does. Like the addict who self-medicates with drugs or the alcoholic who escapes life through drink, we run to victimhood to make ourselves feel better. The belief that we're not responsible for our actions gives us a buzz, or a temporary relief, before dropping us down lower than before.

It's like eating a chocolate-covered razor blade—it tastes sweet at first, but after you swallow it, the chocolate wears off and the razor is exposed.

You see, victimhood is a vicious thing; it takes and tortures its prisoners. Unaware that the belief is the thing that is hurting us and halting us, we will continue to blame anything and everything around us—even our own bodies—but certainly not ourselves.

And so it is with Dante's Satan. Blaming others for his misfortune, he sits at the bottom level of hell, trapped in a prison of his own making.

Although we are certainly not like the "fallen angel" of Dante's *Inferno*, we can pull some powerful, personal lessons from his imprisonment.

Often, we may feel trapped, isolated, beaten down, and defeated. We may feel like our lives are pure hell. But in those moments, we must realize this one, powerful truth: we *do* have the power to stop "beating our wings" (or fists) at our problems. Again, we cannot always control what happens to us, but we can always control how we react. And more often than not, it is our reaction to the situation that liberates us—or damns us.

To get out of your own personal hell, you must recognize that you are a person of worth and that you have an inherent power to persist and strength to move forward. No matter what you might be tempted to think, there is *always* someone out there who believes in you. Use that belief in you to light a fire of belief in yourself. Believing in yourself will free you from stagnation and light the way forward.

Use the following affirmation as encouragement:

> *I choose to live by choice, not by chance.*
> *I choose to make changes, not excuses.*[2]

We are always free to choose—to act and not be acted upon. The sooner we embrace this belief and accept our responsibility, the sooner we will triumph over our circumstances and become a victor instead of a victim.

# 2

## Focus on What You Can Do

Now, after discussing all that, we probably need to talk about our "yeah, buts." You might have read all that Dante/damnation stuff and said to yourself, "*Yeah, but* I really can't do that thing because [insert convincing reason as to why you can't do that thing]."

You might say, "Yeah, but I physically can't do that." Or you might say, "Yeah, but I just don't have enough education." Or you could say, "Yeah, but I've made too many mistakes." Or "Yeah, but I'm mentally and emotionally broken—I'm damaged goods."

Admit it, you have a "yeah, but."

It's OK—everyone has a "yeah, but."

Well, here's my "yeah, but."

I struggle with chronic, genetic depression, which can often be debilitating and heart-wrenching. Depression runs in my family, and it would be easy for me to use that factor as a means to push away from others and blame my circumstances. And for many years, that's exactly what I did.

But to be perfectly honest, those were the most difficult times of my life. It wasn't until I felt a moment of empathy in the wilderness that I began to see my way forward.

## A Lesson in the Wilderness

I used to hate hiking and camping with my whole soul. (Is there any way to emphasize that without using expletives?) But in my early twenties, my struggle with depression became so severe that my dad suggested I work at a wilderness therapy program for at-risk youth in Arizona. And for some reason that remains unknown to me, I agreed.

*I don't know what I was thinking.*

This wilderness therapy program wasn't like camping with family and friends (you know, the kind that gives you a warm fuzzy). This was trailblazing, bushwhacking, backbreaking hiking in the sunbaked desert—without the slightest hint of civilization for miles.

On my first day of work, I swear my trainer led our group through everything I could *possibly* be allergic to (for which she expressed zero remorse).

On my second day of work—after a grueling hike to the summit of a mesa—I came to the conclusion that it was my trainer's intention to kill me. It was the only way to explain a hike that was seemingly inspired by *The Hunger Games*.

At the end of the day, I crawled under my shelter, curled up into the fetal position, and prayed for the sweet release of death. Then it started to rain. It was almost as if God were underscoring my pathetic situation.

*This was day two of eight.* Before us lay another fifteen to twenty miles through a harsh and unforgiving stretch of desert.

I couldn't do it. I physically couldn't do it. I was chubby, allergic, unfit, and inexperienced. To top it off, I was a pasty-white kid from Alaska. I wasn't built for these desert conditions!

Curled up underneath my shelter, shaking with pain and frustration, I couldn't see the way forward. I didn't believe I could do it.

But then my trainer, Xela (pronounced "Shayla"), offered me some encouragement. Crouching down next to my shelter, she asked me how I was doing. I grumbled a number of phrases that thinly veiled my discomfort.

She quietly nodded, and we sat in silence for a few minutes. Then, instead of offering me trite words of encouragement, she said something radically different.

"I know, it sucks," she said.

I furrowed my brow. "You think so, too?"

"Oh yeah. Hiking in the heat, the bugs, the water, the weight of the pack—it's hard. Especially your first couple of weeks."

"So it gets better?" I asked.

She shrugged. "It's *always* hard," she said. "But now it's more—*understandable.* I've made it through the hikes before. I know that they don't last forever. I know that I'll make it out of the canyon because I've made it out of other canyons. I know that I'll eventually climb the mountain because I've climbed other mountains. And tonight? I know I'll make it through this rain—because I've done it before. You'll make it through this, Seth."

It was a moment of empathy that transformed my experience. It didn't lessen the pain, by any means. I was still incredibly sore and suffering from severe allergies. But something inside me responded to Xela's belief that I was going to make it. All I had to do was keep moving forward, small step by small step.

Perhaps many of our struggles can be compared to hiking in the wilderness. *It's never easy.* In fact, the most exhilarating and worthwhile hikes are filled with blood, toil, tears, and sweat. But in the midst of our greatest pains we can find comfort and encouragement in the fact that others with similar struggles have successfully gone before us. Like my trainer Xela, I've learned that the path forward isn't easy, but it can become understandable as we learn from the lives of others.

Likewise, I know that if you continue to move forward—however slow your pace might seem—you will conquer your darkest canyons and your tallest mountains.

As for me, I can attest to a marvelous, inexplicable power that has come to me whenever I've resolved to move forward—in spite of the obstacles. When I truly believe that I have some control over my circumstance, then in that moment I'm given strength to face my demons. It hasn't been easy, and it hasn't been a onetime event. I have to continually reassert my belief that I have control over my life—that I am not helpless and hopeless.

This process of taking ownership of my life and circumstances has always been worth the fight. In a quote attributed to author Robert Louis Stevenson, he said: "In each of us, two natures are at war—the good and the evil. All our lives the fight goes on between them, and one of them must conquer. But in our own hands lies the power to choose—what we want most to be, we *are*."[1]

# 3

## Can't vs. Can

One of the most important steps to overcoming obstacles is changing one's language. Out of a desire to help other people move forward, I've often written about my struggles with depression on my blog. Because of this willingness to be open, I get a lot of emails from people asking for help, and I give advice whenever possible. Every now and then, I'll get pushback emails splattered with one of my least favorite words in the English language—*can't.*

> *I can't do that. I just can't. I've already tried and failed.*
> *I can't. I can't talk to anybody. I can't overcome this.*
> *I can't believe that things will ever get better. I can't.*
> *I can't. I can't. I CAN'T!*

And in the end, I have to agree with them. They *can't* do it. But it's probably not because they're physically unable to do it; instead, it's because their disbelief prevents them from seeing any alternative.

They might put forth some minimal effort to convince other people that they're trying, but inside they've already decided that whatever they can do will not work. Whatever their doctor, their therapist, their friend, or a book says simply isn't going to work, because they've already decided that it won't work.

To be clear, I'm not talking about having doubt. I'm talking about cold, hard disbelief. Doubt contains some measure of faith, while disbelief is the total and absolute lack of hope. The doubter is willing to cautiously hike a new trail, while the disbeliever refuses to believe there even *is* a trail.

Or it's like a person who has a medical problem but doesn't believe in the power of doctors or medicine. This person can complain about his symptoms, sincerely desiring relief, but if he refuses the medicine simply because he doesn't believe it will work, it's very unlikely that he will be healed.

Or it's like a person who believes that she can't run a marathon. If she doesn't believe that she could ever run a marathon, she probably never will. Why would she? She would be too skeptical to sign up, let alone train for one.

I could tell you over and over and over again that you can do this or accomplish that, but my encouragements are all meaningless unless you believe them.

In his book *No Excuses*, Brian Tracy makes this excellent point:

Now, how can you tell if your favorite excuse is valid or not? It's simple. Look around and ask, "Is there anyone else who has my same excuse who is successful anyway?"

When you ask this question, if you are honest, you will have to admit that there are thousands and even millions of people who have had it far worse than you have who have gone on to do wonderful things with their lives. And what thousands and millions of others have done, you can do as well—if you try.[1]

If you want to move forward in life, the first thing you need to do is replace *can't* with *can*. No matter how bad things might seem, you *must* become an optimist about your situation. As Winston Churchill once said, "For myself I am an optimist—it does not seem to be much use being anything else."[2]

"But what if I literally can't?" you might ask. "What if I'm not using my situation as an excuse?" That's a perfectly valid question. The man who has lost his right arm is certainly not making an excuse when he says that he can't write with his right hand.

The woman who has a paralyzing fear of heights is not making an excuse when she says that she can't climb a ladder to get something on the edge of the roof. And the man who is uncomfortable in front of crowds is not making an excuse when he says that he's probably not the best person to give a presentation.

In those legitimate situations, I would ask you to consider focusing on what you *can* do instead of what you *can't* do. The man who is missing his right arm can't write with his right hand, but perhaps he can learn how to write with his left hand or use a computer. The woman who has a fear of heights doesn't need to climb a ladder to get whatever is on the edge of the roof; she can use something to help dislodge it or even ask for help. The man who is uncomfortable in front of crowds can create a presentation that draws the focus of the audience on the media presented rather than on himself.

Perhaps we can't spend millions on humanitarian efforts, but we *can* use our social media capital to spread the word about a good cause. Perhaps we can't express our sympathies in the most eloquent way, but we *can* render simple service that helps lift the burden of another. Perhaps we can't offer healing medicine to someone who is suffering, but we *can* offer our heartfelt empathy.

As we strive to replace *can't* with *can*, there may be instances when what we want to do is very different from what we can do. In those situations, what we can do may seem ineffectual. But seen from a larger perspective, doing what we can do may actually turn the tide in our own personal battles.

Such was the case with the starving orchestra of Leningrad.

# 4

# The Leningrad Symphony

I t was the summer of 1941, and the Nazis were tearing through Russia, destroying everything in their path. Adolf Hitler pompously declared that by August 9, 1942, he and the Nazis would celebrate the taking of Leningrad (the present-day St. Petersburg) in the city's Hotel Astoria.

By early September, the Nazis had surrounded Leningrad, blockading the city and cutting off its main arteries for food, supplies, communication, and reinforcements. But the city's three million inhabitants (which included roughly four hundred thousand children) refused to surrender. Thus began an 872-day siege of catastrophic death and famine. By the war's end, the number of deaths in Leningrad outnumbered those who died in Hiroshima and Nagasaki, *combined.*

In the midst of such hellish conditions, the orchestra of Leningrad planned a counteroffensive. Instead of focusing on what they couldn't do, they focused on what they could do. And what could they do? *They could make music.*

In 1942, the remaining members of the orchestra resolved to perform the newly completed Symphony No. 7 by Dmitri Shostakovich, a native of Leningrad, and broadcast it—on loudspeakers—toward enemy lines.

The score—both long and complex—called for a ninety-piece orchestra, and only half of the members of the Leningrad orchestra had survived the horrors of the siege. And despite extra rations, many of the musicians fainted from exhaustion during rehearsals. They had strength enough to play through the whole piece only once—three days prior to their big performance.

The performance itself was on August 9, 1942—the very day on which Hitler had planned to celebrate the capture of Leningrad.

In her book *Leningrad: The Epic Siege of World War II, 1941– 1944*, Anna Reid wrote, "On the morning of the concert... General Govorov mounted a special Operation Squall, so as to prevent disruption from air raids or barrages. Inside the grandee-packed auditorium the performance itself was ragged, but the atmosphere was overwhelming. 'Some wept,' remembered a woman in the audience."[1]

In an interview, Kseniia Makianovna Matus, an oboist in the Leningrad orchestra, shared her recollection of the symphony's grand finale: "When the piece ended, there was not a sound in the hall—silence. Then someone clapped at the back, then another, then there was thunder. It was improper to embrace, but we wanted to."[2]

Karl Eliasberg, the director and conductor of the symphony, said, "People stood and cried.... They knew this was not a passing episode but the beginning of something. The hall, the homes, the front, the whole city was one human being seizing his victory over the soulless [Nazi] machine. And *we had it, in the music*" (emphasis added).[3]

Long after their triumphant performance, Matus related a remarkable account that Eliasberg had shared with her:

Several years later, after the war was over, the Board of Directors sent for Karl Il'ich and said: "Karl Il'ich, some

Germans are here and they want to meet you." "Me!" he said. "They tried to kill us! So many people died, so many horrible things." He was half German, half Jewish. But they said to him: "Karl Il'ich, it's an order." So someone was told to accompany him, and he went to the Astoria. He sat down and was then approached by some men from a nearby table.

"Karl Il'ich, hello. We are very glad to meet you and we want to express our gratitude."

"For what?"

"For the symphony. We were sitting not far from you, in the trenches. We were bombing you, and the planes were flying—our airfield was there. After all, we had orders to destroy Leningrad. But we sat in a trench and listened to your symphony. And we burst into tears and realized: "Whom are we bombing? We will never be able to take Leningrad because the people here are selfless." [4]

When I get really discouraged, I often think about the Leningrad orchestra. They were starving, dying, and surrounded by forces that wanted to destroy them. And yet, in the face of such hellish evil, they chose to focus on what they could do. Instead of thinking "We're not soldiers, we can't fight back" or "Everything is against us, we can't win," they focused on "can."

"We *can* play music."

Think of it! Instead of curling up in a corner and giving up on life, they played music. And as baffling as it may seem to historians and military generals, *their music* was a force that helped to turn the tide of the war. Focusing on the things we can't do will defeat us. Focusing on the things we can do will lead us to victory.

There can be no miracle without belief. In a very real way, belief is the fuel of miracles.

Consider what would happen if we believed in the encouragement and advice of others. What if, instead of constantly tearing ourselves down, we believed the best about ourselves? What if we believed that we could achieve our dreams, and then worked to do so? Imagine the power of these beliefs!

Instead of focusing on the impossible, focus on what is possible. Instead of giving added attention to what you can't do, give strength and power to what you can do. I promise that doing so will turn the tide in your favor as you battle your way forward.

5

# Transforming a Curse into a Blessing

The first thing you must realize is that your biggest problems can actually be your greatest blessings. The sooner you understand and embrace that truth, the sooner you will gain strength to overcome your challenges.

In his book *The Road Less Traveled*, M. Scott Peck uses the Greek myth of Orestes and the Furies to demonstrate how some of our greatest struggles can become some of our greatest blessings.

Orestes was the grandson of Atreus, a man who had viciously attempted to prove himself more powerful than the gods. Because of his crime against them, the gods punished Atreus by placing a curse upon all his descendants. As part of the enactment of this curse upon the House of Atreus, Orestes' mother, Clytemnestra, murdered his father and her husband, Agamemnon. This crime in turn brought down the curse upon Orestes' head, because by the Greek code of honor a son was obliged, above all else, to slay his father's murderer. Yet the greatest sin a Greek could commit was the sin of matricide. Orestes agonized over his dilemma. Finally, he did what he seemingly had to do and killed his mother. For this sin the gods then punished Orestes by visiting upon him the Furies, three ghastly harpies who could be seen and heard only by him and who tormented him night and day with their cackling criticism and frightening appearance.

Pursued wherever he went by the Furies, Orestes wandered about the land seeking to atone for his crime. After many years of lonely reflection and self-abrogation Orestes requested the gods to relieve him of the curse on the House of Atreus and its visitations upon him through the Furies, stating his belief that he had succeeded in atoning for the murder of his mother.

A trial was held by the gods. Speaking in Orestes' defense, Apollo argued that he had engineered the whole situation that had placed Orestes in the position in which he had no choice but to kill his mother, and therefore Orestes really could not be held responsible. At this point Orestes jumped up and contradicted his own defender, stating, "It was I, not Apollo, that murdered my mother!" The gods were amazed. Never before had a member of the House of Atreus assumed such total responsibility for himself and not blamed the gods. Eventually the gods decided the trial in Orestes' favor, and not only relieved him of the curse upon the House of Atreus but also transformed the Furies into the Eumenides, loving spirits who through their wise counsel enabled Orestes to obtain continuing good fortune.[1]

Consider this: Because Orestes was willing to accept responsibility for his lot, his former curse became his greatest blessing! Everything given to us in life can be either a blessing or a curse. It is the strength of one's heart that determines which it is.

If you feel like your life is hell—*great!* Because within your unique situation is the power for you to transform your life. Seen from the right perspective, the opposition you face can actually make you stronger and wiser.

Touching on this topic, C. S. Lewis wrote:

> That is what mortals misunderstand. They say of some temporal suffering, "No future bliss can make up for it," not knowing that Heaven, once attained, will work backwards and turn even that agony into a glory.... What seemed, when they entered it, to be the vale of misery turns out, when they look back, to have been a well; and where present experience saw only salt deserts, memory truthfully records that the pools were full of water.[2]

You can turn a curse into a blessing, a prison into a palace, and hell into heaven. But how?

## PART 2

# *Unstuck*

## Guides

In his famous 1875 poem "Invictus," William Ernest Henley penned these immortal lines: "I am the master of my fate / I am the captain of my soul."

I wholeheartedly agree. *You* are the master of your life. You, *not your past or your circumstances,* are the author of your life. At any given moment, you have the ability to decide, "This is not how my story is going to end."

But there's more: in addition to being able to control your future, you have the ability to rewrite your past.

Sound a bit far-fetched? Read on.

Some of the most remarkable individuals in history are those who have used their difficult circumstances to their advantage.

Instead of seeing their circumstances as insurmountable challenges, they've used them as stepping-stones to move forward. Instead of believing in the problems of their past, they've "rewritten" those problems to guide others.

In his *Inferno*, the poet Dante was guided through the nine circles of hell by Virgil, a fellow poet and one of Rome's greatest authors. The need of a guide is crucial to our success in life.

To escape our own personal prisons, we need guides—inspirational figures who have walked a similar road and can help us find the way forward. And just as Dante walked through several distinct levels of hell, there are several distinct areas in our lives in which we frequently feel damned. With the help of a guide, we must overcome each of these levels in order to step out of darkness and into the sunlight.

## A Guide for
## Past Mistakes

Do you feel confined in the prison of your past? Do you feel that you've made one too many mistakes? Have your mistakes been so serious that you've had to serve time in prison? Do you feel that your past is preventing you from moving forward?

If so, then I would like to introduce you to an extraordinary man. In his youth, he was known as a troublemaker, and later he became a leader in a revolutionary movement against his country's oppressive government. He was captured, charged with four counts of sabotage and conspiracy to overthrow the government, and imprisoned for twenty-seven years.

While in prison, he memorized the poem "Invictus," which reads, in part,

> *It matters not how strait the gate,*
> *How charged with punishments the scroll,*
> *I am the master of my fate,*
> *I am the captain of my soul.*

Instead of blaming the government, his captors, or his circumstances, this man accepted responsibility for his life and fully believed that he still had power to make a difference.

The man was Nelson Mandela, and he emerged from prison a different kind of revolutionary—one whose attitude of forgiveness would change the world. At the age of seventy-five, he was elected president of South Africa, and his attitude and policies helped disarm and dismantle apartheid's legacy of hatred and racism.

You may feel stuck in life because of your past. You may feel that your mistakes are too great or feel overwhelmed in a prison of your problems. But the life and accomplishments of Nelson Mandela force us to reconsider our possibilities: no matter our past, our circumstances, or even our age, we still have power to overcome by moving forward. Mandela once said, "I am fundamentally an optimist. Whether that comes from nature or nurture, I cannot say. Part of being optimistic is keeping one's head pointed toward the sun, one's feet moving forward. There were many dark moments when my faith in humanity was sorely tested, but I would not and could not give myself up to despair. That way lay defeat and death."[1]

Don't defeat yourself by giving up to despair—keep moving forward.

A Guide for

# Physical Limitations

"But what if I'm physically *unable* to move forward?" you might ask. "What if I have a physical limitation that prevents me from making my body work the way it should?"

This goes back to the discussion of *can't* versus *can*—if you can't move forward in the way that you want, look for ways in which you *can* move forward. As Martin Luther King Jr. once said, "If you can't fly, then run; if you can't run, then walk; if you can't walk, then crawl; but whatever you do, you have to keep moving forward."[1]

In the arena of physical limitations, I would introduce you to two different guides, both of them men who lost the ability to walk. One of them forced his legs forward and eventually regained his ability to walk. The other never regained his ability to walk, but he continued to move forward in his own way. The result? They became giants among men and stepped into eternity.

One of them was a man by the name of Glenn Cunningham. When Glenn was the tender age of eight, his legs were severely burned in a tragic accident at his school. After examining his legs, the doctors suggested amputation, but his parents refused. The doctors offered a grim forecast of Glenn's future, predicting that the child would never walk normally again.

But as he wrote in his book *Never Quit*, Glenn soon found his determination:

One afternoon a stout lady from Elkhart paid Mother a visit.... The visitor had a loud voice. When she prepared to leave, I could still hear her talking outside. "You may as well face it, my dear," she told Mother. "Glenn's going to be an invalid the rest of his life."

When Mother returned, the look on my face told her I'd heard. She came over to the bed and sat down carefully on the edge of the mattress.

I hurled the words at her. "I'm not going to be an invalid. She's wrong, you know! Wrong, you hear?"

Mother reached out, brushed back my hair from my sweaty forehead. She leaned over and kissed me on the cheek. "Yes, Glenn, I know she's wrong." The words came soothingly, gently.

"I will walk again?"

"Yes, Glenn, you'll walk again."

"I will!" And now I was screaming. "I will! I will!"[2]

After years of retraining himself, Glenn was eventually able to walk and run again. In time, he competed in the 1932 and 1936 Olympics, won numerous medals, and set world records for running the mile. He later penned these lines: "You will never reach any higher than you aim, so set your goals high, then endeavor to reach them with honor and integrity—and never give up."[3]

But not all physical limitations are overcome in a similar way. Not all victories are marked by achievements in sports.

In 1921, while enjoying the new heights of a promising political career, a thirty-nine-year-old man contracted the dreaded disease known as polio and became paralyzed from the waist down.

He was devastated. Just one year earlier, he had campaigned for the vice presidency of the United States. And now—what? How could he face down political opponents from a wheelchair? How could he face the world? How could he move forward?

The man was Franklin D. Roosevelt. And in his book *Looking Forward*, he offered this profound insight: "There are many ways of going forward, but only one way of standing still."[4]

Determined to move forward, Roosevelt continued to pursue his political dreams, eventually becoming president of the United States, elected to an unprecedented four terms, during which he led the United States through the Great Depression and World War II.

Consider the incredible irony! Confined to a wheelchair though he was, here was a man who stood tall during a time of great trouble and stood against the evil of Nazi Germany.

If you feel confined by your physical limitations, search for ways in which you can move forward. Let your faith in yourself overpower your doubts. For as President Roosevelt wrote, "The only limit to our realization of tomorrow will be our doubts of today. Let us move forward with strong and active faith."[5]

## A Guide for
## Economic Limitations

"But people like President Roosevelt were rich and privileged!" you might say. "They came from wealthy families and had access to a host of resources and connections. I could never do the things that they've done because I'm not rich or well-known. I'm a nobody."

If you believe that you can't move forward because you lack economic resources, then I would introduce you to a boy named Ben. Born in 1706, he was the fifteenth child of an impoverished candle and soap maker. Ben attended school for about two years but did not graduate. With no connections other than their own, Ben's parents sent him to become an apprentice to his brother James, a printer.

Ben worked for James for about five years, learning everything he could about the trade, reading books, and formulating his own thoughts and opinions. After being denied the opportunity to publish his own writings, Ben developed a pen name (Mrs. Silence Dogood) and submitted them anonymously to the newspaper (i.e., to his brother). Surprisingly, James not only enjoyed what "Mrs. Dogood" had written but decided to publish it. Mrs. Dogood's letters became very popular, filling young Ben with confidence in his own abilities.

At age seventeen, he ran away to Philadelphia. There, broke and homeless, he worked several odd jobs, all of them in the field of printing and publication. With his aim fixed on becoming a master in the publishing world, Benjamin Franklin quickly rose to the top level of society. His success in publishing led him to many other accomplishments, and within his lifetime, this once-impoverished child became the first ambassador of the United States, a man who was as comfortable in the presence of royalty as he was in the presence of merchants and farmers.

The life and writings of this candle-maker's son help light the way forward. Among his many wise words is this simple yet powerful sentence: "Instead of cursing the darkness, light a candle."

At any point in his life, Franklin could have "cursed the darkness" and given up. "I'm too poor," he could have said. "I'm a nobody," he could have thought. "I don't have any education, experience, or connections. I can't do this!" he could have exclaimed.

But instead of cursing the darkness, Franklin lit a candle and continued to move forward—step by step. Countless are the men and women who used what little resources they had to create overwhelming opportunities.

However, I feel that a word of caution should accompany Benjamin Franklin's story of success: "Money has never made man happy, nor will it," said he. "There is nothing in its nature to produce happiness. The more of it one has, the more one wants."

Money, and the want of it, carries as much potential to damn as it does to enable. There are, of course, far more important things than financial gain—things like family and close, healthy relationships.

Furthermore, financial gain is one of the quickest ways to induce the envy of others. Which is probably why Franklin said, "If a man empties his [money] into his head, no one can take it from him." Meaning, as we pursue financial liberation and security, we should invest a sizable portion of that money into educational opportunities. For "an investment in knowledge pays the best interest."

## A Guide for
## Educational Limitations

But perhaps you feel that your educational background *is* your stumbling block. Perhaps you feel that you've had a poor education or that it's too late for you to start learning something new. You might even be tempted to think that your limited knowledge prohibits you from making meaningful contributions.

Two guides will obliterate that kind of thinking.

If you feel damned by a poor educational background, then I would introduce you to Frederick Douglass, an escaped slave who went on to become one of America's greatest authors and orators, and a leader of the abolitionist movement.

After Frederick was taught the alphabet at age twelve, his owner disapproved any more education for him, believing that if a slave learned how to read, he would desire freedom. It seems that he and Frederick shared this belief. "Knowledge is the pathway from slavery to freedom," he would later say; and following this pathway, he taught himself—in secret—how to read and write.

His pursuit of knowledge, in the face of overwhelming obstacles, paved the way for the literal and intellectual freedom of millions—both black and white.

But if you feel that it's too late for you to learn something new, I would introduce you to Helen Keller. When she was nineteen months old, she contracted an illness that left her both deaf and blind. For the next six years of her life, Helen lived in a wordless world, unable to understand that every object she encountered had a corresponding name. In 1887, a dedicated teacher by the name of Anne Sullivan was hired by the Kellers to instruct Helen in communicating through sign language. To do this, Anne identified objects by signing individual words into Helen's hand.

Unable to grasp the purpose behind motions being forced into her hand, Helen grew so frustrated with her instructor that she broke her doll. Then, one day, Helen suddenly realized that the sign language spelling the word *water* in her hand was a symbol for the idea of the water that was running down her other hand.

After this breakthrough in communication, Helen nearly exhausted Anne, demanding to know the names of all the other objects in her world.

Even though she had lost some of her most valuable, formative years of learning, the floodgates of Helen's mind had opened, and knowledge began to pour in. She went on to earn a bachelor's degree and then become a political activist, a lecturer, and a prolific author. Her persistence in spite of her perceived "limitations" still serves as an inspiration to millions. After accomplishing what many would deem impossible, Helen Keller wrote this: "Be of good cheer. Do not think of today's failures, but of the success that may come tomorrow. You have set yourselves a difficult task, but you will succeed if you persevere; and you will find a joy in overcoming obstacles. Remember, no effort that we make to attain something beautiful is ever lost."[1]

# A Guide for
## Mental and Emotional Struggles

But suppose your struggle is much deeper than past mistakes, or than physical, economic, or educational problems. Perhaps you struggle with a mental illness or emotional struggles. Perhaps you're overwhelmed with intense feelings of fear and doubt. Maybe all you want to do is give up.

If that's the case, then I would introduce you to one of my own personal guides. There isn't a day that goes by when I don't think about him and look to his example. (Indeed, I have a large poster of him in my office.)

My guide through life has been, and will ever be, Sir Winston Churchill (1874–1965), the former prime minister of the United Kingdom. His active and steadfast resistance to Adolf Hitler, and his vehement refusal to even consider defeat, helped inspire his nation to victory against Nazi Germany. His strength of character and his determination to never give up—even in the most dire circumstances—has made him one of the greatest leaders the world has ever known.

But despite all his accomplishments, Churchill struggled with what he called "the black dog" of depression. In studying his life—his victories and defeats, his emotional obstacles and personal challenges—I am perpetually amazed by his indomitable will to fight his way forward.

Of his battle with depression, psychiatrist Anthony Storr said this: "Only a man who knew what it was to discern a gleam of hope in a hopeless situation, whose courage was beyond reason, and whose aggressive spirit burned at its fiercest when he was hemmed in and surrounded by enemies, could have given emotional reality to the words of defiance which rallied and sustained us [during World War II]."[1]

In a speech delivered to the House of Commons on June 4, 1940, Churchill rallied his beleaguered nation with these words: "We shall go on to the end. We shall fight in France, we shall fight on the seas and oceans, we shall fight with growing confidence and growing strength in the air, we shall defend our island, whatever the cost may be. We shall fight on the beaches, we shall fight on the landing grounds, we shall fight in the fields and in the streets, we shall fight in the hills; we shall never surrender."[2]

Consider the context of these lines: not only was Churchill leading the charge against Nazi Germany, but also he was simultaneously leading the charge against his own personal depression.

With this in mind, one of his most famous phrases has even more power: "Never give in—never, never, never, never, in nothing great or small, large or petty, never give in except to convictions of honour and good sense. Never yield to force; never yield to the apparently overwhelming might of the enemy."[3]

I'd like to pause here and be completely candid with you. While writing this book, I have felt discouraged many times. The process of creating it has brought to mind many thoughts, feelings, and experiences. Some of those experiences have been good ones, but most of them have been very difficult to remember. Writing this book has made me feel despondent, depressed, insecure, and insufficient. After all, who am I? Who am I that the world should care what I have to say?

But in these moments of self-doubt, I have looked to my poster of Churchill. He doesn't look back at me. Instead, he looks forward, into some distant horizon, as if to say, "Never give in. Keep moving forward."

Throughout my life, I have looked to that stubborn, iron-willed prime minister, and he has always inspired me forward. And although he passed away more than twenty years before I was born, his example continues to influence my life.

The men and women we revere the most are the individuals who refused to be a victim of their circumstances; they took responsibility for how they reacted to the things that were given to them. By taking responsibility for their life, these individuals were able to transcend their circumstances in a most beautiful way.

Find the guide that will lead you forward on your path. Often, if we are determined to move forward, the painful opposition we face in life is the very thing that will make us stronger.

※

# Liberation

In all my talk of damnation and hell, I would miss the mark if I didn't write about liberation and heaven.

The author Nathaniel Hawthorne (1804–1864) was a brilliant American author who often wrestled to find deeper meanings in religious symbolism. In his classic works such as *The Scarlet Letter*, *The House of the Seven Gables*, and *Young Goodman Brown*, Hawthorne demonstrates a clear understanding of how people can damn *and* liberate themselves.

In one of his lesser-known stories, "The Man of Adamant: An Apologue," Hawthorne tells of Richard Digby, a selfish man whose "plan of salvation was so narrow, that, like a plank in a tempestuous sea, it could avail no sinner but himself."

So fixated on his own salvation was Richard Digby that he abandoned his community and traveled into "the dreariest depths of the forest." After journeying "three days and two nights, [he] came, on the third evening, to the mouth of a cave."

There, he declared, "Here my soul will be at peace; for the wicked will not find me.... Of a truth, the only way to Heaven leadeth through the narrow entrance of this cave—and I alone have found it!"

Dark and gloomy though it was, the cave contained an almost magical secret. The water that dripped from its ceilings "seemed to possess the power of converting what it bathed to stone. The fallen leaves and sprigs of foliage, which the wind had swept into the cave, and the little feathery shrubs, rooted near the threshold, were not wet with a natural dew, but had been embalmed by this wondrous process."

Hawthorne reveals to the reader that Richard had, prior to leaving his community, "contracted a disease, for which no remedy was written in their medical books. It was a deposition of calculous particles within his heart, caused by an obstructed circulation of the blood, and unless a miracle should be wrought for him, there was danger that the malady might act on the entire substance of the organ, *and change his fleshly heart to stone* [emphasis added]. Many, indeed, affirmed that the process was already near its consummation."

Disbelieving his deadly diagnosis, Richard moved into the "tomb-like" cave and "allayed his thirst with now and then a drop of moisture from the roof, which, had it fallen anywhere but on his tongue, would have been congealed into a pebble."

For three days, he lived in the cave, "eating herbs and roots, drinking his own destruction, sleeping, as it were, in a tomb, and awaking to the solitude of death."

Towards the end of the third day, he was greeted at the mouth of the cave by a young woman named Mary Goffe. "She had been a convert to his preaching of the word in England, before he yielded himself to that exclusive bigotry, which now enfolded him with such an iron grasp, that no other sentiment could reach his bosom." Mary looked on Richard with "a mild and pitying expression, such as might beam from an angel's eyes."

Richard commanded her to leave, but she would not. She told him that she heard "a grievous distemper had seized upon his heart; and a great Physician hath given [her] the skill to cure it."

Once again, Richard commanded her to leave, but "[a]ll her zeal was for his welfare."

"'Come back with me!' she exclaimed, clasping her hands— '*Come back to thy fellow men; for they need thee, Richard; and thou has tenfold need of them* [emphasis added]. Stay not in this evil den; for the air is chill, and the damps are fatal; nor will any, that perish within it, ever find the path to Heaven.'"

Richard ignored her, opened up his Bible, and fixed his eyes on the page. "The [shadow of night] had now grown so deep, where he was sitting, that he made continual mistakes in what he read, converting all that was gracious and merciful into denunciations of vengeance and unutterable woe, on every created being but himself."

With an "unselfish sorrow," Mary Goffe hastened to a bright fountain and scooped a portion of its water into a cup of birchen bark. She returned to the cave, knelt at the feet of Richard, and offered him the cup of water.

"[D]rink of this hallowed water, be it but a single drop! *Then, make room for me by thy side* [emphasis added].... Do this, and thy stony heart shall become softer than a babe's, and all will be well."

But Richard, in utter abhorrence of the proposal... eyed her with such a fixed and evil frown, that he looked less like a living man than a marble statue, wrought by some dark-imagined sculptor to express the most repulsive mood that human features could assume.

With hatred in his heart, Richard knocked the cup out of her hand, "thus rejecting the only medicine that could have cured his stony heart....

"Tempt me no more, accursed woman," exclaimed he, still with his marble frown, "lest I smite thee down also! What has thou to do with *my* Bible?—what with *my* prayers?—what with *my* heaven [emphasis added]?"

No sooner had he spoken these dreadful words, than Richard Digby's heart ceased to beat; while—so the legend says—the form of Mary Goffe melted into the last sunbeams, and returned from the sepulchral cave to heaven. For Mary Goffe had been buried in an English churchyard, months before; and either it was her ghost that haunted the wild forest, or else a dreamlike spirit, typifying pure Religion.[1]

The tragic story of Richard Digby illustrates a profound truth: the ultimate form of damnation comes to us when we choose to isolate ourselves from others. For just as isolation contains some terrible, damning magic that ended Richard Digby's life, there is a wonderful, liberating magic that comes from serving and loving others.

Every day, we are confronted with situations that invite us to leave the cold and callous confinement of our caves and exercise our humanity for the welfare of others. Life is filled with innumerable Mary Goffes. They come to us not as angels but as everyday, seemingly average people.

The venerable C. S. Lewis put it this way: "There are no ordinary people. You have never talked to a mere mortal. Nations, cultures, arts, civilizations—these are mortal, and their life is to ours as the life of a gnat. But it is immortals whom we joke with, work with, marry, snub, and exploit—immortal horrors or everlasting splendors."[2]

Like Mary Goffe, these immortals reach out to us every day, asking us to "make room for [them]" and offering us the only medicine that can cure our stony hearts: "Come back to thy fellow men; for they need thee... and thou has tenfold need of them."

For if hell is cold, dark, and lonely, then surely heaven is warm, bright, and filled with life! The quickest and surest way out of our own personal hell is to reach out and help someone who is suffering—for in lifting another person, we also lift ourselves.

In *A Christmas Carol* by Charles Dickens, this is the lesson that the ghost of Jacob Marley tried so desperately to teach Ebenezer Scrooge. While Jacob lamented the opportunities he had lost to help his fellow man, Scrooge tried to comfort his friend by telling him that he had been "always a good man of business....

"'Business!' cried the Ghost, wringing its hands again. '*Mankind was my business* [emphasis added]. The common welfare was my business; charity, mercy, forbearance, and benevolence, were, all, my business. The dealings of my trade were but a drop of water in the comprehensive ocean of my business.'"[3]

Heaven, it seems, is populated by people like Mary Goffe: women and men who have a zeal for the welfare of others. According to the Gnostic Gospel of Philip, "In this world, the slaves serve the free. In the Kingdom of Heaven, the free will minister to the slaves." As strange as it may seem to you and me, loving service is the only path to true freedom.

In this book, I have offered you numerous examples of individuals who moved beyond their own "personal damnations." I have detailed their difficulties and described their victories.

But to be honest, I care less about those who are lifted up by society and more about those who lift up society. I am less impressed with their accomplishments and more impressed with what they did for those who were struggling to move forward.

The very nature of a guide is to lead someone else forward. The guides that I have shared with you aren't guides because of what they did for themselves—they're guides because of what they did for *others*.

After setting numerous world records in running, Glenn Cunningham was ideally poised to make a small fortune through product endorsements and a lecture circuit. Instead, he and his wife, Ruth, bought 840 acres of land and opened a youth ranch dedicated to providing farm work and animal husbandry as therapy for troubled children. Glenn and Ruth devoted the remainder of their lives—thirty years—to helping thousands of at-risk youth.

In 1927, nearly six years after being paralyzed by polio, Franklin D. Roosevelt organized the Warm Springs Foundation, in Warm Springs, Georgia. His foundation helped create the first hospital dedicated to treating polio patients and became instrumental in the fight against the dreaded disease. As often as his duties allowed, Roosevelt dedicated much of his time and energy to helping those who had been stricken by polio, offering them hope and encouragement. Tender and heartwarming are the pictures of him among the patients of Warm Springs. It was there, in 1945, that FDR suffered a major stroke and died—among the people he had loved and served.

Frederick Douglass escaped the bondage of slavery and dedicated his life to liberating others. Helen Keller became a political activist and campaigned for labor rights and women's suffrage.

But this cycle of service isn't limited to the historically famous. I know women who were abused as children but refuse to remain the victims of their abusers. Instead, they offer hope, help, and guidance to others in similar situations, and actively work to prevent the abuse of other children.

I know a man who, when he was a child, was beaten by his father and eventually placed in foster care. He has refused to remain a victim of his father's negligence and abuse and has chosen instead to become a loving husband and a caring father.

I know a young woman who was born with cerebral palsy, which severely limited her ability to walk. But she went on to chase her dreams and earn a degree, and she currently works in the district attorney's office in a large city. In recent years, she has been contacted by numerous groups and organizations to speak and motivate others to move forward.

I'm not asking you to do great, historically significant deeds. I'm asking you to do very simple things. For, like small seeds, small deeds can make a big difference.

Benjamin Franklin rose from extreme poverty to become one of America's wealthiest people—but he never forgot his roots. America's first ambassador was prodigiously charitable. In fact, he essentially invented the concept of "paying it forward." In a letter to Benjamin Webb, Franklin wrote this:

> I do not pretend to give such a deed; I only lend it to you. When you...meet with another honest Man in similar Distress, you must pay me by lending this Sum to him; enjoining him to discharge the Debt by a like operation, when he shall be able, and shall meet with another opportunity. I hope it may thus go thro' many hands, before it meets with a Knave that will stop its Progress. This is a trick of mine for doing a deal of good with a little money.[4]

Do you think Benjamin Franklin ever imagined that the concept of paying it forward would still be in use today? Probably not. It was a small, seemingly simple act of service that has snowballed into an unstoppable force for good.

Never doubt your capacity to do good in the world. Never doubt that your contributions, however small, will make a difference.

In my book *Your Life Isn't for You*, I wrote about how seemingly small things can make a big difference: "I once heard someone compare our lives to the wheel of a wagon. He said that when we are at the top of the wheel, we should reach down and lift those who are below us. Then, when they reach the top, they will reach out and lift us. This is the only way in which we can truly move forward in life—by reaching out and lifting another."[5]

Abandon the idea that you will forever be the victim of the things that have happened to you. Choose to be a victor. Embrace that belief, and the frozen lake of your situation will begin to thaw, and you will find a way out. And as you continue to move forward, reach out and lift someone else. For as we lift and inspire other people, we also lift ourselves, and the truest measure of our own freedom is demonstrated by our dedication to liberate and lift others.

As you do so, you will be walking in the footsteps of those heroic guides who have gone before. Continue moving onward and upward, and you will find yourself in the liberating light of heaven.

# Notes

## Part I

### 1 By the Beating of Our Own Wings

1. Dante Alighieri, *The Inferno of Dante: A New Verse Translation, Bilingual Edition*, trans. Robert Pinsky (New York: Macmillan, 1997).
2. From "The Choice Is Mine," attributed to Alexander Starr, in Arnetha F. Ball and Ted Lardner, *African American Literacies Unleashed: Vernacular English and the Composition Classroom* (Carbondale, IL: Southern Illinois University Press, 2005), 95.

### 2 Focus on What You Can Do

1. Robert Louis Stevenson, *Strange Case of Dr. Jekyll and Mr. Hyde* (London: Longmans, Green & Co., 1886).

### 3 Can't vs. Can

1. Brian Tracy, *No Excuses! The Power of Self-Discipline* (New York: Vanguard Press, 2010), 3.
2. Richard Langworth, ed., *Churchill by Himself: The Definitive Collection of Quotations* (New York: PublicAffairs, 2008).

### 4 The Leningrad Symphony

1. Anna Reid, "The Leningrad Symphony," in *Leningrad: The Epic Siege of World War II, 1941–1944* (New York: Walker & Co., 2011), 362.

2. Ed Vulliamy, "Orchestral maneouvres (part two)," *Observer*, http://www .theguardian.com/theobserver/2001/nov/25/features.magazine57 (accessed August 4, 2014).

3. Ibid.

4. Cynthia Simmons and Nina Perlina, "Memoirs and Oral Histories," in *Writing the Siege of Leningrad: Women's Diaries, Memoirs, and Documentary Prose* (Pittsburgh: University of Pittsburgh Press, 2002), 151.

## 5 Transforming a Curse into a Blessing

1. M. Scott Peck, "Grace and Mental Illness: The Myth of Orestes," in *The Road Less Traveled: A New Psychology of Love, Traditional Values, and Spiritual Growth* (New York: Simon & Schuster, 1978), 293–94.

2. C. S. Lewis, *The Great Divorce* (New York: Macmillan, 2001, orig. pub. 1946).

## Part II

## A Guide for Past Mistakes

1. Nelson Mandela, *Long Walk to Freedom: The Autobiography of Nelson Mandela* (Bath, England: Windsor, 2004).

## A Guide for Physical Limitations

1. "Martin Luther King, Jr. Delivered an Assembly Series Address at Washington University in 1957," Washington University in St. Louis, Assembly Series, http://assemblyseries.wustl.edu/past/MLK.html.

2. Glenn Cunningham and George X. Sand, "I Will Walk Again," in *Never Quit* (Lincoln, VA: Chosen Books, 1981), 46–47.

3. Cunningham and Sand, "Dedication," in *Never Quit*, i.

4. Franklin D. Roosevelt, *Looking Forward* (New York: John Day Co., 1933).

5. U.S. National Park Service, "Quotations," Franklin Delano Roosevelt Memorial, http://www.nps.gov/frde/photosmultimedia/quotations.htm (accessed July 17, 2014).

## A Guide for Educational Limitations

1. Helen Keller, address to the American Association to Promote the Teaching of Speech to the Deaf, July 8, 1896.

## A Guide for Mental and Emotional Struggles

1. "Winston Churchill and His 'Black Dog' That Helped Win World War II," National Alliance on Mental Illness, http://www.nami.org/Content/NavigationMenu/Not_Alone/Winston_Churchill.htm (accessed May 2, 2014).
2. Winston S. Churchill, *Never Give In! The Best of Winston Churchill's Speeches* (New York: Hyperion, 2003).
3. Speech given at Harrow School, Harrow, England, October 29, 1941, quoted in *Churchill by Himself: The Definitive Collection of Quotations*, ed. Richard M. Langworth (New York: PublicAffairs, 2008), 23.

## Liberation

1. Nathaniel Hawthorne, *Complete Short Stories* (Garden City, NY: Hanover House, 1959).
2. C. S. Lewis, *The Weight of Glory* (London: Society for Promoting Christian Knowledge, 1942).
3. Charles Dickens, *A Christmas Carol and Other Christmas Stories* (New York: Popular Pub., 2001).
4. "Pay it forward," *Wikipedia*, last modified August 26, 2014, http://en.wikipedia.org/wiki/Pay_it_forward.
5. Seth Adam Smith, *Your Life Isn't for You: A Selfish Person's Guide to Being Selfless* (San Francisco: Berrett-Koehler Publishers, 2014), 39.

## Acknowledgements

I want to express my gratitude to my wife—not only for her constant, loving support, but also for leading me to San Francisco and encouraging me to take an internship at Berrett-Koehler Publishers.

While that internship has blessed my life in numerous ways, I am most grateful for the people I've met and the friends I've made as a result of being an editorial minion. I express my heartfelt gratitude to Jeevan Sivasubramaniam for being my mentor and friend (and for creating the cover art of this book!). You are a giant among men, with awesome socks.

I am grateful for the contributions of Neal Maillet, Charlotte Ashlock, Alyssa Mary DiMaio, Rick Wilson, Dianne Platner, Courtney Schonfeld, and Michael Crowley. I'm also thankful to Leigh McLellan for the amazing design of the book.

I'm profusely and profoundly grateful for my copy editor, Elissa Rabellino—seriously, she's like the Leonardo da Vinci of copyediting!

I'm deeply indebted to the brilliant insight and thoughtful encouragement of Anna Leinberger. Anna possesses a remarkable gift for editing and can turn feathers of inspiration into something that can actually fly.

Finally, I'd like to acknowledge Sir Winston Churchill and Nathaniel Hawthorne, my two favorite authors. For years, their words have quietly guided me through the darkest times of my life—for which I'm sure they'd appreciate some type of acknowledgment.

## About the Author

Seth Adam Smith is an Alaskan-born writer who has had international acclaim. In 2013, his blog post "Marriage Isn't for You" received more than 30 million hits and was translated into nearly twenty languages. A survivor of a suicide attempt in 2006, Seth has learned that true healing comes from focusing on others and sharing "the northern lights of life." He frequently writes about these topics on www.SethAdamSmith.com, www.ForwardWalking.com, and www.HuffingtonPost.com.

## Berrett–Koehler
## Publishers

**Berrett-Koehler** is an independent publisher dedicated to an ambitious mission: *connecting people and ideas to create a world that works for all*.

We believe that to truly create a better world, action is needed at all levels—individual, organizational, and societal. At the individual level, our publications help people align their lives with their values and with their aspirations for a better world. At the organizational level, our publications promote progressive leadership and management practices, socially responsible approaches to business, and humane and effective organizations. At the societal level, our publications advance social and economic justice, shared prosperity, sustainability, and new solutions to national and global issues.

A major theme of our publications is "Opening Up New Space." Berrett-Koehler titles challenge conventional thinking, introduce new ideas, and foster positive change. Their common quest is changing the underlying beliefs, mindsets, institutions, and structures that keep generating the same cycles of problems, no matter who our leaders are or what improvement programs we adopt.

We strive to practice what we preach—to operate our publishing company in line with the ideas in our books. At the core of our approach is stewardship, which we define as a deep sense of responsibility to administer the company for the benefit of all of our "stakeholder" groups: authors, customers, employees, investors, service providers, and the communities and environment around us.

We are grateful to the thousands of readers, authors, and other friends of the company who consider themselves to be part of the "BK Community." We hope that you, too, will join us in our mission.

### A BK Life Book

This book is part of our BK Life series. BK Life books change people's lives. They help individuals improve their lives in ways that are beneficial for the families, organizations, communities, nations, and world in which they live and work. To find out more, visit **www.bk-life.com**.

## Berrett–Koehler
## Publishers

Connecting people and ideas
to create a world that works for all

Dear Reader,

Thank you for picking up this book and joining our worldwide community of Berrett-Koehler readers. We share ideas that bring positive change into people's lives, organizations, and society.

**To welcome you, we'd like to offer you a free e-book.** You can pick from among twelve of our bestselling books by entering the promotional code BKP92E here: http://www.bkconnection.com/welcome.

When you claim your free e-book, we'll also send you a copy of our e-newsletter, the *BK Communiqué*. Although you're free to unsubscribe, there are many benefits to sticking around. In every issue of our newsletter you'll find

• A free e-book
• Tips from famous authors
• Discounts on spotlight titles
• Hilarious insider publishing news
• A chance to win a prize for answering a riddle

Best of all, our readers tell us, "Your newsletter is the only one I actually read." So claim your gift today, and please stay in touch!

Sincerely,

Charlotte Ashlock
Steward of the BK Website

Questions? Comments? Contact me at bkcommunity@bkpub.com.

Certified

Corporation®

bcorporation.net

CPSIA information can be o
Printed in the USA
BVOW07s0857060115

382135BV00001B/6/P

9 781626 563469